EXPLORING HUMAN BEHAVIOUR IN GROUPS

I0165097

A. John Allaway

1971

MONOGRAPH SERIES NO. 4

The Institute for Cultural Research

ISBN 978-1-78479-350-0

First published 1971
Published in this edition 2019

Requests for permission to reprint, reproduce etc., to:
The Permissions Department
ISF Publishing
The Idries Shah Foundation
P. O. Box 71911
London NW2 9QA
United Kingdom
permissions@isf-publishing.org

In association with The Idries Shah Foundation

The Idries Shah Foundation is a registered charity in
the United Kingdom
Charity No. 1150876

About the Author

A. JOHN ALLAWAY was Professor of Adult Education in the University of Leicester.

This monograph is a transcript of a lecture delivered to the Institute for Cultural Research on 12 December, 1970.

Exploring Human Behaviour in Groups

THIS IS IN a way a progress report. It is an account of what has been attempted during the past fourteen years by several different bands of associates of which I have been a member. These have in every case come from different professional backgrounds, some being social psychologists, other psychiatrists, still others sociologists or educationists. In this report I attempt to survey a variety of what were originally experimental ventures some of which have now become, in a measure, institutionalised but not, I hope, fossilised, others having as yet to prove themselves. Perhaps a truer description of them, for me at least, would be that they have been and still are adventures, adventures in the study of intra- and inter-group relationships and transactional behaviours and the exploration of ways in which the learnings gained through their study may be brought to bear upon everyday living, in the home, in the work situation and in leisure-time activity which is social in character.

The study of inter-personal and inter-group relations, of transactional behaviours, is not, of course, anything new. This, in one way or another, is the aim of all the social sciences – of sociology, social psychology and social anthropology, or politics and even of economics. Drawing upon the findings of these sciences it would have been possible for us to have given courses of lectures, using an inter-disciplinary approach, to help people examine the kinds of relations or transactions which they as persons, or the groups to which they belong, enter into. By this means we could have provided our audiences with what William James, in his book *Pragmatism* (Longmans, Green, 1949, p.333) calls knowledge *about* inter-personal and inter-group relations and transactional behaviour. But, whilst not decrying this kind of knowledge, what we were looking for was some way of enabling our students – most of them business and professional people with no wish to become social scientists as such – to gain, using once more the language of James (p.329), knowledge *as acquaintance* in our spheres of interest.

We were not, of course, unaware that some people can convert knowledge about into knowledge *as acquaintance* through active use of the imagination. By this means they can internalise what has been external and make it a part of themselves, so that what John Henry Newman, in his *Grammar of Assent* (Burns & Oates, London, 1870, p.78) calls only a *notional* apprehension of something heard or read becomes *real*. But most of us, we realised, are not highly gifted that way. What comes to us in the form of ideas or concepts does so in an inert state, and in his book *The Aims of Education and other Essays* (Williams & Norgate, London, 1947), A.N. Whitehead warns us (p.1) of the danger of inert ideas, that is to say, ideas which are merely received into the mind without being utilised or tested or thrown into fresh combinations .... Education with inert ideas is not only useless; it is, above all things, harmful.

Following this up Sir Richard Livingstone, in his famous little book *The Future in Education* (C.U.P. 1941, pp. 30–31) speaks of ideas being plastered on the minds of school pupils and university students. We who began these ventures into inter-personal and inter-group relations training were getting a little tired of being plasterers. We wanted to find a way by means of which our students could acquire knowledge directly and not through intermediaries such as ourselves, to get their knowledge *experientially* or by acquaintance. At this juncture we came to hear of 'T-Groups', that is, Training Groups which were being used in the United States for the study of inter-personal relations in the 'here and now', especially at the Gould Academy, Bethel, in the State of Maine, and our interest was at once aroused.

T-Groups, consisting of about fifteen members each, together with a Trainer constituted the basic units in a wider two to three weeks residential course in Group Dynamics. They met daily four or five times until towards the end of the course, the primary task of their members being to engage in inter-personal relations and to examine these as they happened. Into this inter-personal relationship the Trainer did not overtly enter. What he did, or at least tried to do, was to sense what was taking place within the group in terms of social process and endeavour to communicate this to its members, employing for the purpose ordinary everyday language. Towards the end of the course the T-Groups were disbanded, and differently constituted Application Groups took their place. A staff member was attached to each of these, but his function differed markedly from the Trainer's. It was more like that of a Chairman and Resource Person. These groups had as their primary task the study of how 'learnings' in the T-Groups might be applied in the members' 'back-home' situations.

During the academic year 1956-57 the Tavistock Institute of Human Relations had as a Visiting Professor, Hugh Coffey of the Department of Psychology at Berkeley, California.

Coffey had been very much involved in T-Group Training and the Institute sought and obtained his assistance in planning the first British experiment in this field. The Institute was reluctant, however, to embark upon the adventure alone, and learning of my interest in, and willingness to commit my Department to it, the Institute and the University of Leicester entered into a partnership in inter-personal relations (later adding inter-group relations) training, which lasted for more than a decade. The first joint training course in 'Group Relations' as it was called, a residential event of twelve days' duration, took place in Leicester during September 1957. Its design was very similar to that of the Bethel ventures, but the name T-Groups was dropped in favour of Study Groups.

As has already been mentioned the Trainer in a T-Group is there, not to participate in the overt relationships into which the ordinary members enter, but to try to sense what social processes are taking place within the group and to endeavour to communicate what he senses to the group. This, if he is to be reasonably consistent in his communications, he must do within some framework of social-psychological or social-psychiatric theory. In that highly individualistic society, the United States, every T-Group Trainer seemed to use whatever theory took his fancy, so that even on a single course there might be half a dozen different types of interpretative theory being employed. But here, it was agreed that Study Group Consultants, as we decided to call them, should interpret what was going on in their respective groups in terms of the basic assumption theory of Wilfred R. Bion, a former member of the staff of the Tavistock Institute. This theory Bion had developed through experience in conducting psychotherapeutic groups, that is, groups of people suffering from behaviour disorders.

Bion's theory was first set forth in a series of articles which appeared between 1948 and 1951 in the journal *Human Relations*, and later in book form under the title *Experiences in Groups* (Tavistock Publications, London, 1961). It holds that every human group is simultaneously three groups, a work group which is there to perform a task and as such is rational, time-bound, and conscious, a basic assumption group which is irrational, motivated by near-conscious and unconscious wishes and oblivious of time and consequences and a proto-mental group which is deep in the unconscious of the group's membership, and in which the basic assumptions are, as it were, held in solution. To repeat, every group, and not merely every psychotherapeutic or study group, is at one and the same time a work group, a basic assumption group and a proto-mental group.

The basic assumption group takes three different forms. When the group acts as if it were there to find and follow a leader who will take care of it and somehow almost effortlessly solve all the work group's problems for it – to find and follow, as Bion puts it, a dependent leader – then it is in a state of *ba dependency*. When the group acts as if it were there to find and follow a leader who will mobilise it for flight from or fight against the work group's task, then it is in a state of *ba fight-flight*. And when the group acts as if it were there to find and encourage a couple of its members to 'mate', and somehow produce a means to the work group's salvation, free of any effort on the part of the remainder of the group, then it is in a state of *ba pairing*. What is expected of the leadership of each type of basic assumption group is some sort of magic. Rational solutions within the limits of the work group's task are frequently hard, difficult and sometimes distasteful: hence the resort first to one type of basic assumption group and then another.

The proto-mental group is a kind of underground reservoir, a source from which the various basic assumptions take their rise and to which they also return; what is going on there is hidden from the Consultant – its existence is indeed postulated – and no further attention will be given to it. What the Consultant concentrates upon are the manifestations of the other two types of group, namely, the work group and the basic assumption group. And, with regard to the latter, Bion maintains, and experience seems to corroborate his view, that only one form of basic assumption group is operative at any one time. There can be rapid shifts between states of dependency, fight-flight and pairing, within a group, but when anyone of these is manifest the others are quiescent – they are latent within the proto-mental group.

What I have given are, of course, only the barest bones of Bion's theory of group mentality. In making their interpretations within the framework provided by this theory the Consultants were expected to do more than merely express their sense of the group's now being a dependent group, now a fight-flight group and so forth. They were to draw attention to such processes as selective inattention, splitting and scapegoating, at the time they were perceived to be taking place. In performing his task the Consultant was to feel with his group, but not to be unmindful of the cues provided by it, not so much through what was being said or done as by the *way* in which it was being said or done and by the body language by which it was being supported or denied. His comments about what was going on were to be group-centred. Insofar as he made comments upon individual actions or reactions these were to be limited to cases in which the Consultant had the feeling that the individual was acting or reacting, knowingly or unknowingly, on behalf of the group.

It is not my intention to give an account of the first Leicester/Tavistock Conference, as it was called, in Group Relations. This can be got from a small book entitled *Explorations in Group Relations*, written by two of its staff members, Eric Trist and Cyril Sofer, which was published in 1959 by the Leicester University Press. As can well be imagined it was for all concerned a very anxiety-provoking venture, but it proved sufficiently rewarding in terms of the learning possibilities it opened up to justify the arranging of a second Conference a year or so later. And annually after that time a Leicester/Tavistock Residential Conference was held up to 1968, since when it has become a purely Tavistock Conference. But over the years it underwent many changes. Progressively, those elements in it which did not promote learning by experience – lectures, special interest sessions and so forth – were eliminated and replaced principally by Inter-Group Exercises and Large Group Meetings.

The idea of an Inter-Group Exercise was introduced into Leicester/Tavistock Conferences by Harold Bridger as a result of his participation in a Training Laboratory (as the Americans call their ventures) at Bethel. There the Laboratory membership simulated a Town Council which had on its hands a project whose implementation involved all the Council's various committees. The membership was therefore called upon to divide itself into committees and these were to establish means of communication between themselves to enable the project to be dealt with.

Town Council meetings were given the services of one or more Trainers, and so was each Committee and every delegate meeting that might be arranged. The function of the Trainers, as in T-Groups, was to comment upon the social-psychological processes taking place within the different parts of the Exercise.

In our first Inter-Group Exercise we did not ask the Conference membership to simulate anything. They first met in plenary session and were invited to divide themselves into a number of small groups called Sectors and, having done so, to move into designated Sector rooms in each of which a Consultant had already been placed. Arrived there they were expected to establish relationships with other Sectors, including a small Staff Sector, with the object of deciding how two blank sessions in the Conference programme should be filled and to make arrangements for filling them. At the same time they were to study as they happened the inter-group processes in which they were involved. In any inter-sector meetings that were arranged the meeting was given the services of a Consultant.

The role of the Sector and Inter-Sector Consultants was similar to that of the Consultants in Study Groups, except that the Consultant was now expected to try to sense what was happening in his own Sector or Inter-Sector meeting as the happenings there were being conditioned by a number of reference groups, that is, by other Sectors in the Exercise, or by an Inter-Sector meeting. Although the earlier Inter-Group Exercises were not without value to the members, it came to be believed, chiefly through the persuasiveness of Ken Rice, now Conference Director, that the Exercise would become a more powerful learning medium if it could be stripped of every task other than those of division into groups in the first instance and later engagement in Inter-Group (or Inter-Sector) relations and in both, of course, study of the processes as they happened. So, the task of devising a programme of activities to fill two blank sessions in the Conference was dropped.

Consultants are not now imposed upon Sectors. They form part of the Staff Group and are on-call to Sectors, which can at any time discharge them, but Inter-Group (or Inter-Sector) meetings have no choice in the matter. They must have a Consultant. Experience has shown that the Bionian framework for the interpretation of ongoing social-psychological processes is insufficiently wide to take in all that happens in Inter-Group (or Inter-Sector) situations. Pending the emergence of a theory comprehensive enough to enable this to be done, Bionian theory has to be supplemented by theoretical notions derived from political science. Nevertheless, inadequate as is our interpretative repertoire, most of us who have had experience of staff roles in recent Inter-Group Exercises have come to believe that these offer perhaps the most potent of learning opportunities of all the different elements in a Leicester/Tavistock type of training course.

As has been stated the first task of the Conference membership in the Inter-Group Exercise is to divide into several Sectors. The number is not prescribed. Usually one more room is made available to Sectors than the total number of Study Group rooms. Never, as yet, has the membership remained seriously to discuss how it should divide itself into Sectors, although in most Conferences a few have tried to persuade it to do so. It has swarmed, as it were, and apparently mindlessly, into the nearest available Sector room until it could take no more, then split up into lesser swarms which have flowed into the remaining rooms, leaving a few stragglers behind. This unpremeditated swarming results in the Sectors being in large measure mere human aggregates, lacking almost entirely any of the characteristics of social groups. As such they are powerless to interact with other sectors. What each has to learn to do is to develop a group sentiment and establish a group boundary (a psychological boundary, that is) and to do so as people drift in from outer space, as it were, or take off into outer space.

Slowly, and by painful experience, the inchoate Sectors learn the need for and develop some sort of structure and then, maybe, become so involved in structural problems as to lose sight of the task of the Exercise – a case of either flight from or fight against it. But as they do, from time to time, try to cope with the task they, in experience, come up against problems of delegation and of trust, present possibilities of rejection, test abilities to tolerate uncertainty and so forth. In this Exercise the Staff Sector can, like any other Sector, seek to promote Inter-Sector meetings of various kinds, but this it rarely does. It tends to limit its activities to sending out messengers to gather from, or convey to, Sectors factual information, or to make staff interpretations to one or more Sectors as to what it feels is currently happening either in a particular Sector or in the Exercise as a whole. If the services of the Consultants on-call are not being made use of, staff interpretations may also be sent to one or more Sectors arising out of this fact.

The notion of including a series of Large Group meetings in a Conference was prompted by difficulties experienced by staff and members alike in plenary sessions. These had invariably proved sticky affairs. The Large Group, consisting of members and staff to the number of about seventy, met in a single room in which the chairs had been arranged in three inward-facing concentric circles. Two Consultants sat almost facing one another in each of the circles and the two or three Observers were located around the outer circle, taking notes of the proceedings. The primary task of the membership of the Large Group was to engage in inter-personal relations within it and to study these as they happened. And the Consultants were there to interpret, within a Bionian framework of theory, what was taking place. Like the Inter-Group Exercise, the Large Group has now become an element in every full-scale Leicester/Tavistock type of Conference or course.

The phenomena which are present in the Study Group appear also in the Large Group. But members bring to the Large Group identifications with their respective Study Groups and this gives it something of an inter-group character. Thus claims and counter-claims on behalf of Study Groups get bandied about from time to time. The Large Group is an anxious group, anxious most of the time. Pressures build up in it for dependent leadership, especially from the Staff, and when this is not forthcoming strong hostility manifests itself. In the Large Group hurtful things are done by individuals and the Group to other individuals without their arousing any compassion for the victims. And, quite commonly, those who do those things blandly deny any responsibility for them. The Large Group presents many learning opportunities to its members as to what happens in assemblies of upwards of thirty people, but it seems that resistances to learning are greater here than in smaller groups.

This brief and inadequate sketch of the main features, as they have evolved over the past thirteen or fourteen years, of Leicester/Tavistock type training courses in Group Dynamics is all that time permits me to give. If anyone should wish to study these in greater detail, he would do well to read Ken Rice's *Learning for Leadership* (Tavistock Publications, London, 1965). From being occasional residential affairs these conferences or courses have become more regular and there are also ventures – such as those held in Northampton, Leicester and Nottingham, during the past six or seven years – on a part-time week-by-week basis. Long before the partnership between the Tavistock Institute and Leicester University was dissolved – an entirely friendly parting I might add – each party had begun to promote conferences or courses on its own. Leicester committed itself very fully to inter-personal and inter-group relations training, and since that time the Grubb Institute of Behavioural Studies and the Universities of Bristol and Nottingham through their Departments of Adult Education, have later entered the field.

As has been indicated more than once the Leicester/Tavistock type of inter-personal, inter-group relations training had as its aim helping the members learn by experience the ways of social groups. Since a great part of our lives is lived in such groups the importance of this kind of training is obvious. But many of the members of our conferences and courses were people whose professional duties involved them with others on a one-to-one, or one-to-two-or-three basis, and here, I felt that the relational dynamics must be somewhat different from those in social groups. I therefore decided to try to organise a group in which the primary task would be to engage in from two to five-handed relationships and to examine these as they happen. The problem was, however, to find a suitable framework of theory within which I, as Counsellor (that is what I had decided to call myself) could interpret what was happening. Fortunately, at this time, I picked up a copy of Eric Berne's *Transactional Analysis in Psychotherapy* (Evergreen Books, London, 1961) and this seemed to give me just what I wanted.

I mentioned to my colleague Professor J. W. Tibble the plans I had in mind for the promotion of what I had decided to call a Transactional Analysis Group, and lent him my copy of Berne's book to read. He agreed that the plans were feasible and we therefore arranged that if the response to invitations to join a Transactional

Analysis Group was sufficient he would counsel a second group. They were, and two groups were therefore established at the University Centre, Northampton four or five years ago. Since that time there have also been Transactional Behaviour Groups, as they are now called, in Leicester and Nottingham, one or two having been arranged in each place most years, and Dr K. Stewart and Mr Joe Richards have served as Counsellors to some of them. As far as I know ours are the only Transactional Behaviour Groups for normal people anywhere.

The Transactional Behaviour Group goes through two different phases of development. In the first it is committed to learning, by more or less traditional methods, the salient features of Berne's theory of transactional behaviour and some of the more common pastimes and games through which this expresses itself. As it gains knowledge of the theory this group is encouraged to apply its knowledge to transactional situations in the 'there and then' brought to the group by its members, situations in which at one time or another they have been involved. This is the stage of *Structural* Analysis – analysis after the event. The next stage is that of *Transactional* Analysis, in which members of the Group engage in transactions with each other, and examine these, from the Bernean viewpoint, as they happen. In the first stage the Counsellor is more like a teacher; in the second he is rather less of an interpreter than is the Study Group Consultant. He does not so much report what he feels to be going on in this dyad, or that triad or tetrad, as ask questions of the participants in any particular series of transactions to stop and examine what they, or rather, what they themselves in particular ego states, are up to. He is thus more like an advocate cross-examining his clients.

According to Berne, two-handed, three- and four-handed transactions take place between persons in one or other of three Ego States, namely, those of Parent, Adult and Child. A person's Parent is his own parents (or parental substitutes) whom he as a child internalised in two forms, that of perceived Nurturing Parent and that of perceived Judgmental Parent; a person's Child is himself as he actually was as a child, and it also appears in two forms, that of the Natural Child, demanding, creative and spontaneous, and the Adapted Child, who is as he perceived his parents as wishing him to be; and a person's Adult is the reasoning, data processing and reality-testing part of himself. The theory maintains that all the while any person is engaged in transactions, he is in one or other of these Ego States, but never in more than one of them at the same time. Shifts in Ego States can, however, be frequent and rapid. Moreover, transactions between persons in their different Ego States can take place at two levels simultaneously, at a social level, that is, overtly and at a psychological level, or covertly.

Normally, Berne tells us, transactional behaviour is not random; it is patterned and the patterns fall into three broad classes. These are operations, pastimes and games, the last constituting elements of life scripts.

'Pastimes and games,' says Berne, 'are substitutes for the real living of real intimacy.' (*Transactional Analysis*, p.86). The spotting of these, as they are being played, and their analysis, are the main functions of the Transactional Behaviour Group. Games are the more important and a game is defined by Berne as follows (*Games People Play*, Andre Deutsch, London, 1967, p.48):

.... an ongoing series of complementary ulterior transactions progressing to a well-defined predictable outcome. Descriptively it is a recurring set of transactions, often repetitious, superficially plausible, with concealed motivation; or, more colloquially, a series of moves with a 'gimmick'. Games are clearly differentiated from procedures, rituals and pastimes by two chief characteristics (1) their ulterior quality and (2) the pay-off.

In the various elements of the Group Dynamics conference or course – Study Group, Inter-Group Exercise and Large Group – the members are given a brief account of Bion's theory, but they learn group dynamics by experiencing them and by internalising their different Consultants or, if you like, their roles. Group dynamics can be learned with only the sketchiest intellectual knowledge of Bion. But, in Transactional Behaviour Groups, the members are first given an opportunity to grasp Berne's theory intellectually. Then, with the aid of a Counsellor, they have the chance to try to validate it experientially and, insofar as they do validate it, it becomes part of the member's very self. The aim in both cases is not increase in intellectual knowledge, although that may take place; it is personality change, in the one case improving the member's skills in participation in intra- and inter-group relationships, in the other leading towards greater openness and honesty in the members' involvements in dyadic, triadic and tetradic situations.

Arising out of experiences gained as a Consultant in Group Dynamics training conferences and courses, and as a Counsellor in Transactional Behaviour Groups, supplemented by knowledge of an intellectual nature of the business consultancy work of the Tavistock Institute of Human Relations, I was emboldened to devise a third type of group which would not be primarily concerned with training its members or changing them, although it could do both. In this type of group the members would be concerned to explore in depth some social-psychological problem, or nexus of problems, with which it believed that it was confronted. I call it an Exploration Group. The first ever organised was for a number of clergy who had asked to be provided with a certain formal course instruction, which I felt sure would not really meet their needs. Its object was to find out from them what lay behind their request. The second was set up to help a group of leading citizens in a large city to examine their attitudes toward adolescents, and the third to assist a fairly large local government department to look at itself with a view to carrying through a thorough reorganisation.

Unlike Group Dynamics Groups and Transactional Behaviour Groups, Exploration Groups do not have as their primary task engagement in intra- or inter-group or transactional behaviour and the study of it as it happens. Their primary task falls into two stages, first, that of definition, that is, definition of the problems which the Group believes it is met to deal with. Then, the problems having been brought to light, sometimes from depths and in forms of which the members had only been barely conscious or even unconscious, entry can take place into the second stage. This consists in examination of the problems as they have been defined and their implications for the Group and for its individual members. The Group may then proceed to a decision on the problems, but whether it does so or not is a matter entirely for itself, for giving assistance to the Group in pursuit of this task is outside the Consultant's remit.

The Counsellor to an Exploration Group does not participate in the interchanges which take place between the Group's ordinary members, except, first, to ask questions directed towards clarification of what he takes to be real issues being tackled by the Group, second, when appropriate, to feed information to the Group or to indicate where such information may be sought, or third, to draw attention to unsophisticated use within the Group of Bionian basic assumptions or to the playing of games by some of the members. In developing the concept of the Exploration Group I have had the help of Professors James Holloran, Arnold Joselin and J. W. Tibble and Mr Colin Bourne, colleagues on the staff of the University of Leicester. The Exploration Group, it will be realised, cannot, like Group

Dynamics Conferences and Courses or Transactional Behaviour Courses, be promoted. You cannot mount one and invite people to take part: you can only have an Exploration Group if and when a number of people say they have a problem and invite your help in dealing with it.

I come now to the most recent of the new ventures in group work with which I have been actively associated. In all but this, the intra- and inter-group relations or the transactional behaviours, which are the subject of study, find expression mainly through the medium of speech. The encounters studied are largely *verbal* encounters. True, as I have pointed out, the words are often accompanied by bodily movements – body language, I have called it – but these play only a minor part, at least in the eyes of the group participants. For some time I had wondered whether it might be possible to design group settings in which the members could learn intra- and inter-group relations and transactional behaviours experientially by non-verbal means. Once again manna dropped as from heaven. Dennis Rice, Warden of Vaughan College, Leicester, on returning from America where he had been introducing Leicester/Tavistock type Study Groups to Fordham University, made me a gift of a copy of William C. Schutz's book, *Joy: Expanding Human Awareness* (Grove Press, N.Y., 1967) and in this I found what I thought I had been looking for.

Schutz is a psychologist who has held senior appointments at Harvard and Berkeley, in the University of California, and is the author of a substantial book *FIRO: A Three-Dimensional Theory of Inter-Personal Behavior* (Reinhart, N. Y., 1958). He has had much experience conducting group dynamics and sensitivity training groups as well as consultancy work with big business concerns. He is now Director of the Residential Programme at the Esalen Institute, Big Sur, California, of which he was one of the founders. The work done there arose out of his asking himself where would the joy of his infant son Ethan go as he grew up. For, 'In most of us,' he says, 'it (the joy) becomes depleted, distorted, contorted. Guilt and fear begin to defile it. Somehow the joy .... goes never fully to return.' (*Joy*, p.10). I doubt whether Schutz has yet found the complete answer to his question, or ever will, but his search for it led to the discovery of ways in which older people could at least recapture some of the joys which once were theirs in childhood. About the ways he discovered Schutz remarks (*Joy* pp.10–11):

> A cornerstone of this approach is honesty and openness. This may sound simple, but it is not. Training people to be direct and not devious, to express their feelings honestly – this is difficult and often fraught with risk, but enormously rewarding. Directness deepens and enriches relationships and opens up feelings of warmth and closeness that are rare in most of our experiences.

He points out that the approach goes against the grain of our culture. It involved *doing* something rather than just talking, which may be useful in seeking intellectually to understand personal experience, but is a poor means for helping a person to *experience* – to feel. He also emphasises the point that the ways he discovered, and which are pursued at Esalen, do not suit the needs of everyone, but that many get from them an enormous sense of release from the unproductive tenseness of much everyday living.

What Schutz did was to devise a series of exercises and activities having as their object either (1) the development of personal functioning, through the sharpening and expansion of the range of the individual's sensory awareness – of sounds and sights and bodily feelings or (2) the development of inter-personal functioning of a dyadic nature and in groups of different sizes, including the Large Group, or both in combination. At the risk of giving a rather one-sided impression of what happens in an Esalen type of interpersonal encounter I will offer one example – there is no time for more. And here, I shall speak as through the mouth of the Trainer:

> Open your eyes and look
> about you.
> When I tell you to do so, move
> about on your haunches,
> and find a partner with
> whom to sit back to back.
> Will you please find your
> partner, now?
> If you cannot find a partner, a
> member of the staff will help
> you to do so. Lean on your
> partner, giving and taking as
> much support as you need.
> Relax your buttocks and
> haunches and explore with

your own back that of your
partner.
Now try to communicate with
him NON-VERBALLY.
Express your feelings through
your back.
Become aware of the rhythms
of breathing – suck in and
blow out.
Can you feel the head,
shoulders, spine? Are you
giving or taking support?
Close your eyes, but continue
relating to each other. Now
(after about four minutes
have passed) slowly open
your eyes.
Rise and face your partner
and non-verbally express
something of your feelings at
that moment towards him.
And now, without words,

thank your partner and take leave of him.

Without direct personal experience I was unwilling to experiment along the lines of the work being done at Esalen, but in July of this year (1970) Joe Richards and I were fortunate in being able to participate in a venture in London, conducted by members of the staff of the Esalen Institute, including Schutz himself. About four hundred people took part in it. My colleague and I were deeply affected by our experience and felt that we must share it with as many people as possible. So we devised a one-day Esalen type of course bearing the title *Expanding Human Awareness*. This, very fortunately, we were allowed to hold on Saturday, 26 September, in the Education Centre at the St Crispin Hospital, Northampton.

The maximum number of places we could offer was forty and all were at once taken up. Our impression of this course is that it succeeded in doing what it was intended to do, at least for many of its members, and Joe Richards and I are under constant pressure to repeat it.

In general it would, I believe, be true to say that the system of education in this and most other countries in the Western world has always been, and still is, strong on the education of the intellect and weak on the education of the emotions, good at equipping people to manipulate ideas and things but poor at helping them to relate meaningfully and positively to each other. This one-sidedness is reflected, so it seems to me, in the stunted personal and social development of so many of its people and more especially of its more highly educated and intelligent people. The kinds of group work with which I have been closely identified for almost a decade and a half has had as its most general objective a restoration of the balance, by helping people to become more aware of, and responsive to, the emotional aspects of the social situations within which they find themselves and to improving their personal and inter-personal functioning therein. Insofar as this can be achieved it should, so it seems to me, enable them, as I believe that it has enabled my colleagues and myself, to give and to get more joy in living.

About Idries Shah

BORN IN 1924 into an aristocratic Afghan family, Idries Shah created a large body of literary work, most of which considered elements of "Eastern Thought", especially Sufism and Sufi thought. Some of his best known works include The Sufis and several collections of teaching stories featuring Nasrudin.

Shah devoted his life to collecting, selecting and translating Sufi books and key works of Sufi classical literature, adapting them to the needs of the West and disseminating them in the Occident.

Called by some "practical philosophy", by others "templates in straight thinking" – these works represent centuries of Sufi thought and Islamic thought aimed at the development of human potential to its fullest extent.

They stress virtues such as commonsense, clear-thinking and humor to counter cant and religious dogma. As such they are vital works in the area of Islamic philosophy, and may be viewed as an antidote to radicalism and fanaticism much needed in the world today.

Shah's books have been translated into dozens of languages, have sold in their millions, and are regarded as a cultural bridge between West and East. His work and contribution to Sufism are represented by The Idries Shah Foundation.

About ISF

ISF IS DEVOTED to championing a sense of imagination, and to teaching stories – the kind of which are contained in the large published corpus of the writer and thinker, Idries Shah.

Engaged in a wide range of charitable projects on a world-wide basis, the Foundation seeks to stimulate the minds of both young and old by regarding the world in new ways.

In collaboration with UNESCO, ISF has begun a major story-writing competition for children in five languages and 180 countries. Other projects are working to give illustrated books to kids in Afghanistan and other conflict zones on a mass scale, thereby sparking the innate sense of imagination in young minds.

Yet another endeavour is striving to build the first global StoryBank – bridging disparate societies through stories – which we regard as the essence of all culture.

Thank you for your support of ISF, and your interest in our projects.

**A list of all the monographs
to be published in the series:**

An Eye to the Future
*Dr. Alexander King, Dr. Martin Holdgate, Eugene
Grebenik, Dr. Kenneth Mellanby, George McRobie*

East and West, Today and Yesterday
*Sir Stephen Runciman, Patrick O'Donovan, Peter Brent,
Sir Roger Stevens, Nirad C. Chaudhuri, Iris Butler, Prof.
G.M. Carstairs, Richard Harris*

Science and the Paranormal
Leonard Lewin, D.Sc.

Sufic Traces in Georgian Literature
Katharine Vivian

Rembrandt and Angels
Michael Rubinstein

Biological and Cultural Evolution
Mary Midgley

The Age of Anxiety: a Reassessment
Malcolm Lader

Goethe's Scientific Consciousnes
Henri Bortoft

The Healing Within: Medicine, Health and Wholeness
Robin Price

A Clash of Cultures: The Malaysian Experience
David Widdicombe, Q.C.

Evaluating Spiritual and Utopian Groups
Arthur J. Deikman, M.D.

The Crusades as Connection: Cultural transfer
during the Holy Wars
Contributed by Cultural Research Services

Baptised Sultans: The contribution of Frederick II
of Sicily in the transfer and adaptation of Oriental
ideas to the West
Contributed by Cultural Research Services

Brain Development During Adolescence and
Beyond
Dr. Sarah-Jayne Blakemore

Collective Behaviour and the Physics of Society
Philip Ball

Counter-Intuition
Dr. Kevin Byron

Music, Pleasure and the Brain
Dr. Harry Witchel

Fields of the Mind
Dr. Rupert Sheldrake

Why do we leave it so late?
David Canter

Scheherazade and the global mutation of teaching
stories
Robert Irwin

Consciousness, will and responsibility
Chris Frith

Extraordinary Voyages of the Panchatantra
Ramsay Wood

www.ingramcontent.com/pod-product-compliance
Lightning Source LLC
Chambersburg PA
CBHW020607030426
42337CB00013B/1250